A Float of
Crocodiles

By Karlie Gambino

Gareth Stevens
Publishing

Please visit our website, www.garethstevens.com. For a free color catalog of all our high-quality books, call toll free 1-800-542-2595 or fax 1-877-542-2596.

Library of Congress Cataloging-in-Publication Data

Gambino, Karlie.
 A float of crocodiles / Karlie Gambino.
    p. cm. — (Animal groups)
 Includes index.
 ISBN 978-1-4339-8195-1 (pbk.)
 ISBN 978-1-4339-8196-8 (6-pack)
 ISBN 978-1-4339-8194-4 (library binding)
 1. Crocodiles—Juvenile literature. I. Title.
 QL666.C925G36 2013
 597.98'2—dc23

                              2012018266

First Edition

Published in 2013 by
Gareth Stevens Publishing
111 East 14th Street, Suite 349
New York, NY 10003

Copyright © 2013 Gareth Stevens Publishing

Designer: Ben Gardner
Editor: Greg Roza

Photo credits: Cover, p. 1 © iStockphoto.com/Alan Smithers; interior backgrounds Daniiel/Shutterstock.com; p. 5 Jason Edwards/National Geographic/Getty Images; p. 7 Uryadnikov Sergey/Shutterstock.com; p. 9 Vladimir Koletic/Shutterstock.com; p. 11 © iStockphoto.com/Сергей Урядников; p. 13 © iStockphoto.com/sombutt kaewjunchai; p. 15 kavram/Shutterstock.com; p. 17 Sergey Starostin/ Shutterstock.com; p. 19 Martin Harvey/Peter Arnold/Getty Images; p. 20 saiko3p/Shutterstock.com; p. 21 Debora Atuy/Flickr/Getty Images.

Printed in the United States of America

CPSIA compliance information: Batch #CW13GS: For further information contact Gareth Stevens, New York, New York at 1-800-542-2595.

Contents

Boldface words appear in the glossary.

Floating with Crocodiles

Crocodiles, or crocs, are **reptiles**. They live in rivers, lakes, and **swamps** in warm places around the world.

A group of crocs is called a float when it's in the water. It's called a bask when the crocs are on land.

Happy Together

Crocodiles like to be with other crocodiles. A float may have mothers, fathers, and young crocs. It may include other crocs, too. In large floats, crocs can often be seen resting next to and even on top of each other.

A Lot of Crocs!

The number of crocodiles in a float depends on how much food is around. The more food there is, the bigger the float. A float can have as few as two crocodiles or as many as 100.

Meat Eaters

Crocodiles eat meat. They hide in water and wait for animals to come near. Quickly, they jump forward and grab the animals with their strong **jaws**. The crocs in a float may work together to catch and eat dinner!

Digging In

Crocodiles live where it gets very hot. They stay cool by lying in water. When the weather is cooler, they dig **burrows** to lay in. The crocs in a float sometimes work together to dig large burrows.

Who's in Charge?

The largest and oldest crocs in a float are in charge. They get to eat first while the others wait their turn. The largest crocs also get the best places to sun themselves and the best burrows.

15

Croc Talk

The crocodiles in a float **communicate** with each other. They move in special ways, and they touch each other. They also use lots of sounds to communicate. Crocs hiss, grunt, cough, growl, and roar!

17

Baby Crocs

Mother crocodiles lay eggs on land. The babies squeak just before breaking out of their eggs. The mother takes care of her babies. She carries them to water in her mouth. Fathers may help care for young crocs, too.

Crocs of the World

Did you know there are 14 kinds of crocodiles in the world? The smallest are dwarf crocodiles. The biggest are saltwater crocodiles. They can grow to be 20 feet (6 m) long! All crocs like living together in floats.

Fun Facts About Crocodiles

Crocodiles have been on Earth since the time of the dinosaurs.

Crocs can live up to 70 years in the wild.

Mother crocodiles can lay up to 90 eggs at one time.

Crocodiles are great swimmers, but they can also run on land.

Glossary

burrow: a hole made by an animal in which it hides or lives

communicate: to share ideas and feelings through sounds and motions

jaw: the bones that hold the teeth and make up the mouth

reptile: an animal that has scales, breathes air, and lays eggs. Turtles, snakes, crocodiles, and lizards are reptiles.

swamp: an area with trees that is covered with water at least part of the time

For More Information

Books

Antill, Sara. *A Crocodile's Life*. New York, NY: PowerKids Press, 2012.

Sexton, Colleen. *The Saltwater Crocodile*. Minneapolis, MN: Bellwether Media, 2012.

Websites

The Crocodile Hunter
www.crocodilehunter.com.au
Learn more about crocodiles and other wild animals on this fun website.

Nile Crocodiles
kids.nationalgeographic.com/kids/animals/creaturefeature/nile-crocodile
Read about the Nile crocodile, see pictures, and watch a video of a mother with her babies.

Index